KNOW HOW KNOW WHY

OUR PLANET

Written by Gordon Volke

Illustrations by Mike Atkinson, Sean Milne & Stephen Sweet

Licensed exclusively to Top That Publishing Ltd
Tide Mill Way, Woodbridge, Suffolk, IP12 1AP, UK
www.topthatpublishing.com
Copyright © 2014 Tide Mill Media
All rights reserved
0 2 4 6 8 9 7 5 3 1
Printed and bound in China

ORIGINS OF EARTH

Our planet is one of eight planets circling the Sun. Our whole solar system is just one of many millions in a vast universe.

How old is Earth ?

 Earth was formed around 4.7 billion years ago

 Dinosaurs arrived around 250 million years ago

 Humans arrived around 200,000 years ago

Imagine 'time' as represented by the distance between your outstretched arms. The universe was formed on your longest left-hand finger. One-cell lifeforms began between your wrist and your elbow. Dinosaurs did not appear until you reach your right hand. Humans arrived on the fingernail of your longest right-hand finger!

How was Earth formed ?

One theory is that Earth formed from a gigantic cloud of spinning gas and dust. Here's what is thought to have happened:

A floating cloud of gas and dust was sent spinning by an exploding star.

Gases formed inside the spinning cloud to form a new star – our Sun.

The remaining dust continued to spin around the Sun, forming the planets.

The planets collided and were sent spinning into their orbits.

MANTLE
This section contains more iron than the crust and is like melted plastic the nearer it gets to the core.

OUTER CORE
This is an incredibly hot 3,700°C (6,692°F). This, plus the inner core, is larger than the planet Mars!

INNER CORE
This section is a solid ball composed mainly of iron. It is the hottest part, at 4,300°C (7,772°F)!

THE CRUST
This section is thickest at the Himalayas (70 kilometres/ 43 miles) and thinnest beneath the oceans (5 kilometres/3 miles).

Was there life on Earth from the beginning

Definitely not! At first, Earth's surface was far too hot to support any form of life. Gradually, however, it cooled down so that a thin crust formed round the outside. It remained boiling hot inside – and is still the same today!

When did life on Earth start

The oldest microfossil found so far is 3,500 million years old. Life began about 1,000 million years after Earth was formed. Scientists tend to date the age of rocks to give us clues to Earth's age, working on a 'calendar' that spans millions of years.

Early life on Earth.

What does Earth look like ?

It was Neil Armstrong, the first man to walk on the Moon in July 1969, who said Earth looked like 'a splendid jewel suspended in space'. That is what it looked like to him from his *Apollo* spaceship. Seen from space, the beautiful appearance of Earth is caused by sunlight reflecting off the oceans. This gives the planet its sparkling blue appearance. Wreaths of cloud appear as swirling white masses, while land covers only about one quarter of the surface of Earth.

Earth as seen from space.

FACT BYTES

The distance round Earth from top to bottom and round the middle is almost the same – 40,000 kilometres (24,860 miles) – it's slightly different because the world isn't exactly round.

Earth is made up of layers. We live on the crust.

THE SUN

Our Sun was formed billions of years ago. All the planets in the solar system orbit around the sun, and it provides warmth and light to Earth. Despite being very old, both the surface of the Sun and its interior are hotbeds of activity.

How big is the Sun ?

The Sun is truly massive. To give you some idea, it is 110 times wider than Earth and you could fit Earth into the Sun about 1,300,000 times! Interestingly, the temperature of the Sun's surface is about the same as at Earth's core.

How hot is the Sun ?

As you would expect from such a gigantic fireball, the temperature is blazing hot. The centre of the Sun is estimated to be around 15 million degrees centigrade (59 million degrees fahrenheit). That's hot enough to melt absolutely anything instantly!

What is the Sun made of and how does it work ?

The Sun started as a rotating cloud of gas and dust. This rotation flattened the cloud and pressed the dust together in the centre so that it became a larger lump. Once enough matter had been pressed together, the lump became larger, very dense (squashed) and very hot! Once the heat reached a certain point, nuclear reactions began and the star, our Sun, was born! The nuclear reactions at the Sun's centre create enough pressure to prevent the Sun collapsing.

SOLAR FLARE

CORONA

CONVECTIVE ZONE

RADIATIVE ZONE

CORE

The Sun started as a cloud of dust and gas and formed a large ball.

After the Sun was formed, dust around it clumped together, forming planets.

Earth relies on the Sun's heat and light to sustain life on its surface.

FACT BYTES

From the earliest times, humans have realised the need for the Sun to sustain life. The Aztecs of ancient Mexico, the Incas of Peru and the ancient Egyptians all worshipped the Sun as a god.

What is the difference between a sun and a star

Nothing! A sun is a burning star that gives out light. So, by looking at the night sky, you can see that the Sun is not alone in being a star. All those twinkling pinpoints of light are other stars in other galaxies, giving out heat and light just as our Sun does!

How long will our Sun last

The Sun will burn out eventually, but don't worry – it's not going to happen just yet. Scientists estimate that the Sun will have used up all its energy in about 7,000 million years time!

What are all those black spots

Sunspots are dark patches on the surface of the Sun. They appear black because these areas are not as hot as the gas surrounding them. Some sunspots are around 150 times larger than Earth! Bright clouds of helium, called faculae, occur above the areas where sunspots are about to form. Solar flares are bright loops of hot gas emerging from the areas of the Sun where sunspots are present. A flare can last from a few seconds to several hours.

THE SUN

Warning

Don't try looking for sunspots or solar flares. You should never look at the Sun through a telescope or with the naked eye. It can damage your eyesight and even make you go blind.

An artist's impression of a cross-section of the Sun.

FACT BYTES

Only a small part of the Sun's total energy reaches Earth, but it is enough to make everything live and grow.

THE ATMOSPHERE

You can't see Earth's atmosphere, but it is the layer between Earth and outer space. It is delicate and under threat from the use of chemicals here on Earth. At present, scientists do not know of any other planet which has an atmosphere like ours.

What exactly is Earth's atmosphere

21% oxygen
0.9% argon
0.03% carbon dioxide
0.07% other gases
78% nitrogen

The special layer surrounding Earth is up to 1,000 kilometres (621 miles) thick and is held in place by Earth's gravity. It is made from many gases, including oxygen and carbon dioxide. Life on Earth depends on this combination of gases.

What are the northern lights (aurora borealis)

Particles heading to Earth from the Sun join together in a ribbon called a solar wind. Some particles become charged and are forced down into Earth's atmosphere where they collide and react with gases. This causes the ions to glow red, violet, green and blue. These displays are most often seen at the Poles (hence the northern/southern lights), where they can occur around 200 times per year!

THE EXOSPHERE
This is the very edge of space. It extends from 450–1,000 kilometres (280–621 miles).

THE THERMOSPHERE
This fourth layer goes from 80–450 kilometres (50–280 miles) above the ground.

THE MESOSPHERE
This extends from 50–80 kilometres (30–50 miles). There is very little water vapour at this height, but lots of important ozone that screens us from harmful sunlight.

THE STRATOSPHERE
This second layer extends from about 12–50 kilometres (7–30 miles). Most planes fly at this height, to avoid any storms or bad weather.

THE TROPOSPHERE
Most of our weather is contained within this first layer. It gets colder the higher up you go and the air also gets thinner. The very top part is called the tropopause.

What is the atmosphere made of

Earth's atmosphere is made up of five different layers – the troposphere, the stratosphere, the mesophere, the thermosphere and the exosphere. If you were an astronaut blasting off in a spaceship, you would pass through these five layers described on the left.

Why is the sky blue

Light is made up of a whole spectrum of colours which blend together. Light also has different wavelengths, the longest of which is found at the red end of the spectrum, with the shortest at the blue end. When sunlight enters the atmosphere, it collides with oxygen and nitrogen atoms which 'scatter' different wavelengths, the shorter, blue ones being the most affected. This results in our perception that the sky is blue.

Why does the sky change colour

At sunrise and sunset, the Sun is very low in the sky. This makes light strike the atmosphere at a different angle, scattering different wavelengths of light. So, at these times of day, the sky appears as beautiful shades of red, yellow and orange.

FACT BYTES

When a space shuttle returns to Earth from orbit, it has to pass through the atmosphere. The heavier air causes the spacecraft to become very hot and heat shields need to be used to prevent it burning up.

THE ATMOSPHERE

WATER

Did you know that the glass of water that you drank today could once have been used to wash Shakespeare's feet? Water is circulated in one of nature's most impressive systems, the water cycle, which is described here.

No water is ever created or lost, just stored in different ways ...

Where does it all start ❓

We can start the cycle by imagining a rain cloud about to burst. The water rushes to Earth, making its first stop at the surface of mountains. Some of it is stored here where it freezes. The rest flows down into streams which become rivers. This river water flows into massive reservoirs where some is taken away by pipes to the water supply works to be used as drinking water. The rivers also take some water to the sea. However, some water collects elsewhere on the ground.

Mountains

FACT BYTES

The largest lake in the world is the Caspian Sea, which has an area of 371,000 kilometres^2 (143,200 square miles) and is bordered by several countries, including Azerbaijan, Russia, Kazakhstan and Iran.

Waste water treatment works

Why are oceans salty ❓

Oceans get salt from Earth's crust.

If you filled a washing-up bowl with water from the sea, it would contain around 450 g (1 lb) of salt. The same amount of water from a freshwater source would contain about 5 g (0.01 lb) of salt! Even though the seas are fed by freshwater rivers, the seas and oceans contain salt from other sources, such as broken up rocks, worn-down mountains and gases that have escaped from Earth's crust. They are ever-present and do not evaporate.

How much water is on Earth

Seventy per cent of Earth's surface is covered by water, most of which is salty and found in the seas and oceans. Only two per cent of the world's water is suitable to drink or to water crops. As most of this is frozen in the ice caps, it's no wonder that we recycle water whenever we can. Water cannot ever be created or destroyed – it just gets stored in different ways.

Water supply works

What happens to water before I drink it

The water we drink is usually taken from rivers by pipes and stored either on the surface in reservoirs, or under the ground. At the water supply works, a substance is added to make any large pieces of dirt stick together, which are then lifted out. The water is filtered again, and chemicals are added before it is pumped along a network of pipes and up through our taps.

The water supply works treat our drinking water.

What happens to the water that we don't drink

Water gets taken to the sea and rivers where the Sun shines on it. This causes some of the water particles to change their shape and form vapour (gas). This gas then rises up into the air (evaporation). When the Sun isn't shining, it takes longer for water to evaporate and disappear. When it's cold, the water stays around as snow.

What causes rain and snow

The water droplets inside a cloud move around and bang into each other, causing them to stick together and get bigger. When they become too heavy for the atmosphere to support their weight, they 'fall out' of the cloud. If this happens when it is warm, the raindrops remain liquid and rain falls. When it's really cold and the droplets get colder on the way down to Earth they freeze to become snow. Water falls in all of its different forms, landing on Earth's surface. This is known as precipitation. We're now back to the beginning of the cycle!

MOUNTAINS

Around 300 million years ago, two supercontinents called Laurasia and Gondwanaland, which had been moving towards each other at a rate of several centimetres a year, crashed, buckling with great force, forming mountains ...

What is a mountain range

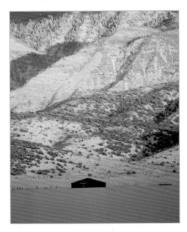

The Rockies, Colorado.

'Range' is the name given to a group of mountains. The Alps make up a range of mountains, passing through six countries in total. The highest point is Mont Blanc (4,807 metres/ 15,770 feet) which is situated between France and Italy.

The Rockies are a range of mountains situated in North America, stretching from Canada to central Mexico. Another mountain range, the Andes, runs 7,242 kilometres (4,500 miles) along the west coast of South America.

How are mountains formed

If you could look inside a mountain, you would see that the rock inside looks bent and crumpled. Fossils found on the tips of mountains are often those of sea animals. These two things make scientists believe that mountains were formed by very powerful forces pushing huge rocks from the seabed upwards to form the mountains. These forces are still moving under our feet, but so slowly that you will never notice!

Which is the highest mountain ?

Mount Everest, in the Himalayas of South Asia, is the highest place on Earth. It is 8,848 metres (29,029 feet) above sea level. Despite its awesome height, the mountain has been climbed many times. Sir Edmund Hillary and his local guide, Sherpa Tenzing, were the first to do so, reaching the summit on the morning of 29th May, 1953.

Hillary (right) and Tenzing.

What are tectonic plates ?

The supercontinents that crashed together formed a single land mass called Pangea. This broke apart to form the continents. These gigantic pieces of Earth's jigsaw are called tectonic plates, which float on top of a layer of magma. Geologists know that the plates still move at several centimetres per year!

FACT BYTES

Geologists believe that the plates of India and Asia were once separated by sea, and that the Himalayas mountain range formed when they drifted together and struck one another. This took place around 600,000 years ago – which makes the Himalayas fairly young!

What is an underwater mountain ?

In some oceans, the tops of underwater mountains poke out above the surface making steep islands. One mountain in the Pacific Ocean, Mauna Loa, is actually much bigger than Mount Everest when measured from the seabed.

RIVERS

All rivers start from high ground, whether they are slow-flowing or torrential. The journey downhill is often a long one, and the river will change direction and size on the way.

What is a river's source

The source of a river is where it begins. The source of the Ganges, a major river in the Indian subcontinent is at the Gangotri Glacier, a massive block of ice situated in the Himalayas.

What is a river's estuary

Huge ports are built around estuaries, where the river flows out to meet the sea. They contain brackish water, a mix of fresh and salt water, and are affected by the sea's tides.

What can we use rivers for ?

Venice's canals provide a water-based transport system.

Ships bring goods inland.

Rivers can be very useful for transporting goods. The River Ohio in America connects Lake Erie with a vast network of inland rivers that bring coal and petroleum products to, and from, America's major cities. Huge loads can be carried on barges which are able to take goods a long way inland.

In certain parts of the world where it is too wet to build roads, rivers are used exactly as roads are, with boats being the replacements for cars. Venice is known as the 'City of Canals' because of its water-based transport system.

River water is used to provide life. Bangladesh sits on approximately 700 rivers, and although floods have negative effects, the silt deposits fertilise the soil and the fish can be eaten as a source of protein.

FACT BYTES

The Amazon was given its name by the Spanish explorers who first sailed up the river in the 16th century. They were attacked by fierce, long-haired tribesmen who they thought were women. So they called them Amazons after the famous female warriors in Greek mythology.

Which is the longest river

The Nile in Africa is the longest – but not by much. It measures 6,650 kilometres (4,130 miles) from one end to the other. Close behind comes the Amazon in South America which stretches for 6,400 kilometres (4,000 miles). The Yangtze in China comes third, followed by the Mississippi–Missouri in North America. These are the world's 'big four' rivers.

The Nile.

How are rivers formed

When rain falls on high ground, or snow melts near the top of a mountain or glacier, the water which can't be soaked up by the ground flows downwards. As time passes, this constant stream of moving water carries the soil away, carving a narrow valley into the ground. This grows wider and wider, deeper and deeper, until a river is formed. It may join other rivers to become larger.

FACT BYTES

The word Mississippi means 'Big River' or 'Father of Waters'. No wonder then, that it stretches 4,070 kilometres (2,530 miles)

What is a river's delta

When a river has been flowing for many years, the mud and stones it brings down build up to make new land. This blocks the flow, making the water split into several streams to get past. In the end, the mouth of the river looks like a hand with lots of fingers. The Ganges delta looks like this.

Rivers begin in mountains and each eventually flows out to sea.

ELECTRIC SKIES

With a bolt averaging a length of 5 kilometres (3 miles) and a temperature four times hotter than the Sun, it is no wonder that lightning is one of the most dramatic of all nature's phenomena.

What causes a thunderstorm

These clouds grow vertically instead of horizontally.

In a word – electricity! Cumulonimbus clouds (see pages 22–23) build up in the sky. These rain-bearing clouds usually produce showers, but they can gather together to produce more serious downpours.

Negatively charged water droplets sink to the bottom of the cloud.

Inside these vast clouds, water droplets form static electricity by swirling around and bumping into each other. The positively charged water droplets gather at the top of the cloud, while the negatively charged ones sink to the bottom.

Electricity (lightning) flashes between the charged droplets.

Eventually, the difference between the positively and negatively charged droplets becomes so great that electricity flashes from one to the other. This is called sheet lightning and it passes through the cloud.

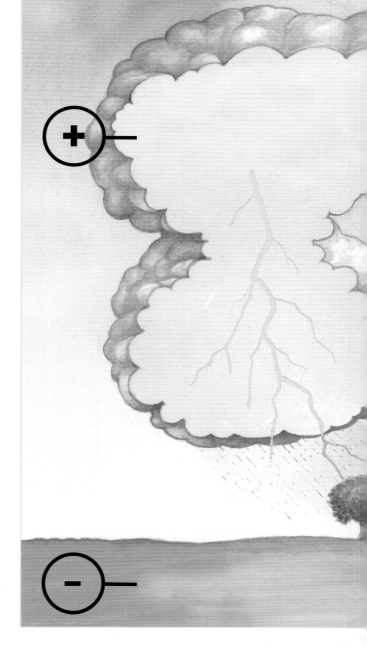

The ground below is also negatively charged, so electricity flashes down from the cloud to the ground. This makes the much more dangerous fork lightning. Finally, these massive discharges of electricity heat up the air inside the storm clouds. The air expands so quickly that it explodes, causing the tremendous rumbling and crashing noise that we call thunder.

Is it safe to get into a car during a storm

A car is one of the safer places to be if you can't get indoors. However, this is not due to the rubber tyres which are commonly believed to insulate you from the ground. (When something is an 'insulator' it means that forces of electricity or heat cannot pass through it very easily.) The reason the car protects you is due to its metal shell. Metal is a conductor, meaning the electricity runs straight through it, taking lightning to the ground. Just make sure you don't touch the metal.

Shelter in a car – but don't touch the metal sides!

Who was Benjamin Franklin

In 1752, American scientist Benjamin Franklin proved that lightning was made of electricity by flying a kite in a thunderstorm. It had a metal key attached to it and the electricity was seen sparking off the end. (This was a highly dangerous experiment and people who tried to repeat it were killed by lightning strikes!)

objects, like trees, are prime targets for a lightning strike.

How far away is the storm

When you see a flash of lightning, count the number of seconds before you hear the following rumble of thunder. If there's a long gap, the storm is a long way away. If it's short, the storm is almost overhead. (If you want to be more accurate, every two seconds is the equivalent of one kilometre / half a mile away.)

ELECTRIC SKIES

FACT BYTES

Light travels much faster than sound. Therefore, we see the flash of lightning before we hear the clap of thunder that it has caused.

EARTHQUAKES

Earth's crust is not a smooth coating like an eggshell but a restless, shifting surface from which huge tremors can come with little warning.

What causes an earthquake

Earth's crust has lots of huge cracks in it which make the land in between look like tiles. These massive sections, called plates, move and rub together, building up pressure. Most of the pressure is absorbed by rocks, but when it gets too much, trouble starts. The plates shatter at their weakest point, releasing enormous amounts of energy which radiate outwards as shock waves, making a large area of ground shake violently. These are called seismic waves. Most damage occurs near the middle of the earthquake which is called the epicentre.

What happens afterwards

Tremors often continue after the main quake, making rescue work even more difficult. These follow-up tremors are called aftershocks. On 12th January 2010, an earthquake measuring 7.0 on the Richter scale shook Haiti in the Caribbean. By the 24th January, at least 52 aftershocks had been recorded.

FACT BYTES

When earthquakes occur under the sea, they cause gigantic waves, called tsunamis, and can cause huge incoming waves (wrongly called 'tidal waves'). Although rare, they can cause massive damage. An earthquake in December 2004 caused an Indian Ocean tsunami, with waves reaching a height of 30 metres (98 feet).

An earthquake occurs when tectonic plates move and rub against one another, building pressure deep within Earth.

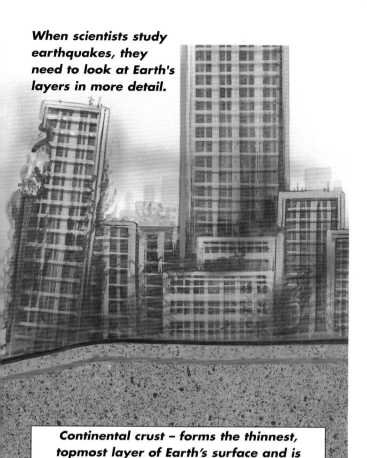

When scientists study earthquakes, they need to look at Earth's layers in more detail.

Continental crust – forms the thinnest, topmost layer of Earth's surface and is mainly rock.

Lithosphere – around 250 km (155 miles) thick, this layer is rigid at the top and softer when it descends into the upper mantle.

Asthenosphere – mainly formed from the upper mantle and is a layer of thick fluid.

How do we measure earthquakes

In 1935, Charles Richter devised a simple scale to indicate the size of an earthquake from 0–10. Anything under 3.5 would not be felt but is recorded. Under 6 would cause slight damage to a well-made building. Over 8 means a great earthquake.

A seismometer is used to measure earthquakes.

Can we predict earthquakes

Not exactly, but scientists who study earthquakes can isolate several warning signs. The normal pattern of seismic waves starts to speed up, and swelling can be detected in the ground. Lots of tiny tremors occur along the junction of Earth's plates. As with volcanoes, it is important to look at the history surrounding the area where earthquakes have happened in the past to try to establish patterns in the size of the 'shocks'. This is one of the reasons that seismologists record even the tiniest tremors that would go unnoticed by us.

What was the biggest earthquake

The largest recorded earthquake took place in Chile in 1960, measuring 9.5 on the Richter scale. One of the most deadly earthquakes took place in the Mediterranean in 1201 killing over one million people. Most of the world's earthquakes occur in a zone known as the Pacific Plate.

VOLCANOES

Volcanoes are a constant reminder of the awesome power of the molten magma that sits just 40 kilometres (25 miles) below Earth's surface.

What makes a volcano erupt

Just 40 kilometres (25 miles) beneath our feet, Earth is a bubbling mass of liquid rock so hot it will melt anything it touches. This molten rock is called magma. Most of the time Earth's crust keeps this magma well underground, but sometimes it finds one of those faults in the crust. Then it has a chance to escape! Magma from inside Earth is subject to enormous pressure. It is also full of explosive gases. So when it finds a weak spot (usually between two plates), it surges upwards and gushes out into the air with terrific power.

For how long do volcanoes continue to erupt

When a volcano often erupts, it is called active. The world's most active volcano is Kilauea on the island of Hawaii. Eruptions started in January 1983 and show no sign of slowing down. If a volcano hasn't erupted for a long time by human standards (perhaps several hundred years) but still could do so, it is said to be dormant. The Mexican volcano, Paricutin, erupted between 1943 and 1952 and has been dormant ever since. If a volcano has definitely finished erupting and won't do so again, it is extinct. The city of Edinburgh in Scotland is located on an extinct volcano. The geographical conditions have changed so greatly since the event (during the Carboniferous Period, about 250,000,000 years ago) that there is no danger that it will erupt again!

What is lava

Underneath Earth's crust is a layer of hot liquid rock called magma. When it spews from the top or the sides of a volcano, we call it lava. At first, it has the texture of melted plastic, but it gradually cools and turns to solid rock.

Lava ... liquid to solid.

What are the world's most famous volcanoes

Lava erupts through top

Lava flows through sides

Magma finds a weak spot.

You may have heard of some of these terrifying natural events.

The ruins of Pompeii.

Mount Vesuvius, Southern Italy
This volcano had an elevation of 1,281 metres (4,203 feet) and famously erupted in 79AD, wiping out the ancient Roman city of Pompeii.

Mount Etna, Sicily
This dormant volcano is huge and dominates the island of Sicily in the Mediterranean.

Krakatoa, East Java in Indonesia
This volcano erupted in 1883, causing the loudest explosion ever heard in the world. It also set off a tsunami that drowned 36,000 people and caused unusually high tides as far away as Britain!

Mount Pelee, Martinique
The volcanic island of Martinique in the West Indies was subject to an eruption in 1902. It destroyed the town of St Pierre.

Mount St Helens, 'Mountain of Fire', North America
This very active volcano has erupted several times in the last 300 years.

FACT BYTES

Just like earthquakes, volcanoes also occur underwater. The hot lava is soon cooled by the sea, forming pillow-shaped blocks called pillow lava.

Vulcan was the Roman god of fire. So scientists who study volcanoes are known as volcanologists.

THE WIND

As long as Earth keeps turning, there will be wind. Some places in the world experience tornadoes and hurricanes more frequently than others. Wind can cause chaos and destruction, but can also be harnessed to provide energy.

The eye of the hurricane.

Why does the wind blow ?

The movement of air (wind) is caused by two things – differences in temperature on Earth and the fact that Earth is always rotating. The Sun does not heat Earth evenly. Its rays are much more intense at the equator and the surface here is much hotter than at the North and South Poles.

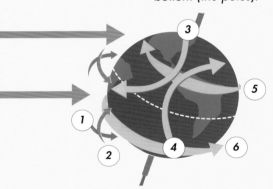

The Sun warms Earth, getting hottest around the equator. Warm air rises to the Poles. (1)

Air blowing from the North Pole causes the wind to blow from north to south (northerly wind). (3)

Westerly and easterly winds blow because Earth never stops spinning. The middle of Earth (the equator) spins faster than the top and bottom (the poles).

Cold air from the poles rushes in to fill the empty space. (2) Wind is caused by temperature and rotation.

Air blowing from the South Pole causes the wind to blow from south to north (southerly wind). (4)

Air travelling towards the equator is pulled westwards (5) and air that is travelling towards the poles is pulled eastwards. (6)

What exactly is a hurricane ?

Hurricanes are storm-force winds that build up over the sea. The moist air rises upwards and cold air rushes in. The strong wind caused by this starts to spin because of Earth's rotation. When this spinning wind builds up, it becomes a swirling monster up to 2,000 kilometres (1,243 miles) across, often reaching speeds of 120 km/h (74 mph).

Hurricanes can cause mass destruction.

What is the eye of a hurricane

In the very centre of a swirling hurricane, there is an area where it is quite calm. The eye of a hurricane can range from 3 km (2 miles) to 370 km (230 miles) across.

What is a tornado

Tornadoes form over land (not water). Rain clouds meet and start to spin as a result of Earth's rotation. These swirling clouds, or 'twisters', form into giant funnel shapes that move along at terrifying speeds – up to 480 km/h (300 mph).

Twisters move at terrifying speeds.

What is the Beaufort scale

This is a scale, invented by a British admiral called Sir Francis Beaufort in 1805, which divides the speed of the wind into twelve graded strengths.

Beaufort number	Wind speed (mph)	Seaman's term	Beaufort number	Wind speed (mph)	Seaman's term
0	Under 1	Calm	6	25–31	Strong breeze
1	1–3	Light air	7	32–38	Moderate gale
2	4–7	Light breeze	8	39–46	Fresh gale
3	8–12	Gentle breeze	9	47–54	Strong gale
4	13–18	Moderate breeze	10	55–63	Whole gale
5	19–24	Fresh breeze	11	64–72	Violent storm
			12	73 or higher	Hurricane force

RAIN

Rain, rain, go away ... once you have read the information on these pages, you will know what kind of rain you can expect simply by looking at the shapes of clouds.

What is rain, and how does it get there ?

Rain is water that has been drawn up into the sky by the Sun's heat and returns to the ground when it cools. This process is called the water cycle. For more on the water cycle, see pages 8–9.

How are rain clouds formed ?

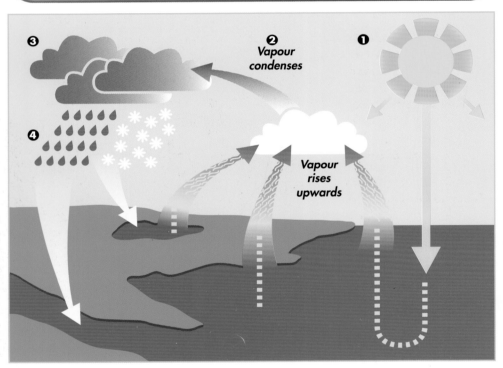

The water cycle.

A rain cloud forms in distinct stages. At stage three, the process happens very quickly and rain can start to fall in a matter of hours!

1. The Sun shines on open water, drawing vapour into the air.

2. As this water vapour rises upwards, it cools down and condenses.

3. Droplets gather together to form clouds, which join together with one another, making bigger and heavier cloud banks in the sky.

4. When the rain clouds become full of heavy droplets, they fall back to Earth in the form of rain (or hail and snow if the air is very cold.)

① *CIRRUS*
The highest clouds of all, made entirely of ice crystals. The strong winds of the upper atmosphere blow these small clouds around, giving them their famous 'mares' tails' appearance.

② *CIRROSTRATUS*
Another ice cloud that can distort the light of the Sun, giving it a coloured halo.

⑧

⑩

③ **CIRROCUMULUS**
*Made of ice crystals,
these high fluffy
clouds often form into
regular-looking ripples
across the sky.*

④ **ALTOSTRATUS**
*High, thin sheets of
cloud that completely
cover the sky and make
the Sun look hazy.*

⑤ **ALTOCUMULUS**
*Puffy-looking rolls
of cloud with dark
sides found at
medium heights.*

⑥ **STRATOCUMULUS**
*These occur when
Cumulus clouds spread
out into wide sheets.
Viewed from above,
they look like a
continuous, flat
carpet of cloud.*

⑦ **CUMULUS**
*Beautiful-looking dense
white clouds that look
like giant cauliflowers!*

⑧ **CUMULONIMBUS**
*The word 'nimbus'
means 'rain' in Latin, so
this type of cloud brings
showers. If they gather
together huge banks,
they can produce
heavy rain and
thunderstorms.*

⑨ **STRATUS**
*A huge dull cloud that
hangs in the air, feeling
like fog and giving a
damp drizzle.*

⑩ **NIMBOSTRATUS**
*Often called 'low cloud'
because it is the closest
to the ground.*

What kinds of clouds are there ❓

There are ten different cloud formations recognised by scientists. They were first classified by an amateur weather expert called Luke Howard who spent his life observing clouds and their different characteristics.

What causes a flood ❓

Floods occur when there is more rain than the ground can absorb. They can also be a result of extra high tides and natural disasters like earthquakes, volcanic eruptions, hurricanes and tornadoes. Global warming also causes flooding, forcing sea levels to rise, swamping any low-lying coastline.

When water has nowhere else to go ...

FACT BYTES

Rainbows occur when rain falls at the same time as the Sun shines. Each raindrop splits the sunlight into its spectrum of colours like a prism. This happens right across the sky, picking up the shape of Earth and giving the rainbow its distinctive curved appearance. A new cloud variety has been recently recognised – called 'undulatus asperatus' – it is awaiting official classification from the United Nations' World Meteorological Organisation.

RAIN

SNOW AND ICE

Snow, like rain, can be a mixed blessing. It provides water when it melts from high ground, homes for both humans and animals, and a fabulous winter playground for children. Yet too much of it can cause chaos, disaster and loss of life ...

What makes it snow

When the temperature of the air below a cloud reaches freezing point or beneath, water droplets in the cloud form ice crystals. When other droplets falling from the cloud bump into the ice crystals, they stick together, forming larger crystals (snowflakes).

What shape are snowflakes

Snowflakes are hexagonal. Large, fluffy flakes are formed when the air below a cloud is slightly warmer than 0°C (32°F), so the falling ice crystals melt slightly, then clump together. If the air around a cloud is constantly 0°C (32°F) or below, then the crystals do not melt and fall in a shower of much smaller flakes – known as powder snow.

As snowflakes melt, they form more 'dendrites' (branches).

How do people live in the cold

The Inuit (native peoples of the Arctic) have turned their natural environment to their advantage, using melted snow for drinking water and building things from ice. Their ice houses (igloos) can be put up in a few hours. The Inuit rely on dogs to pull their sledges great distances. Remains of these dogs, preserved in the snow, show that the Inuit have used these animals for at least 1,000 years.

How are snow and ice different

Snow is made up of snowflakes which have a lot of air in between them. Ice is solid frozen water. You can turn snow into ice by scooping a handful and pressing it together, getting rid of the air.

Where is the coldest place ?

There are many very cold places on Earth – the Arctic, the Antarctic, Greenland, Canada, Siberia in Russia, for example. The coldest temperatures of all (around -90°C / -130°F) are recorded in the Antarctic. The coldest place where people manage to live is in Siberia.

Once an igloo is built, it makes a surprisingly warm home!

What is a blizzard ?

A blizzard occurs when the wind blows at the same time that it is snowing. It makes the snowfall much more dangerous because nothing can be seen in the swirling snow (sometimes called a whiteout). Blizzards also pile the snow up against houses and cars, making it difficult, or impossible, to get out.

When does the sea freeze ?

At the North and South Poles, the sea freezes solid every year and special ships called icebreakers are needed to smash a passage through it. In Europe, very cold weather can make the sea freeze at the edges. Rivers can also gain a thick layer of ice. In fact, years ago, the River Thames in London used to freeze over on a regular basis and a fair used to be held on it. The last of these Frost Fairs took place in February, 1814.

FACT BYTES

Normally, things contract when they are made colder and expand when they warm up. Water, however works the other way around – it gets larger as it gets cooler (which is why ice in your fizzy drink floats and doesn't sink). Scientists think that this is due to water particles having a different shape to other liquids – the molecules in a block of ice are organised in tightly joined patterns which means its volume expands but its density decreases.

SNOW AND ICE

EXTREME HEAT

While one part of the world experiences snow or floods for most of the time, other parts may not experience rain for ten years or more. A town in Chile, South America, experienced the longest drought ever – a staggering 400 years!

Where is the hottest place

Africa, Death Valley in America, and Australia are well-known for experiencing extreme heat. In 1917, the temperature in Death Valley averaged 48°C (120°F) on 43 consecutive days in July and August. Ethiopia has an incredible average temperature of 34°C (93.2°F). This calculation takes into account the freezing night-time temperatures as well as the boiling daytime ones!

ETHIOPIA

What is a desert

A desert is a place that has very little growing in it, mainly due to very low rainfall. Deserts can be classified in four ways. Those found in Ethiopia are true deserts – hot, dry and sandy. Semi arid deserts in Utah are more humid. Coastal deserts, like the Atacama in Chile, have harsh, rocky areas. Cold deserts, like those of Greenland and Antarctica, can experience snow – but usually less than 5 cm (2 in.) per year.

What is a sandstorm

Apart from the blistering heat, travellers in sandy deserts may also experience terrifying sandstorms, where the arrival of gale force winds can lift the sand into huge walls that swirl upwards and fill the sky, blocking the Sun. Sometimes, the force of the sand blowing around is so strong that it can crackle with electricity. Sandstorms can last for hours, smothering people and their belongings.

An oasis in the desert is a welcome sight!

Why is a desert cold at night

This seems like a puzzle, but has a simple explanation. There are very few clouds in the sky above a desert, so there is nothing to screen the Sun's heat. Without them, the ground warms up very quickly, but at night it loses its heat because there are no clouds above to trap the warmth. The Sahara experiences temperatures of 54.5°C (130°F) during the day, but is freezing at night.

What is an oasis

An oasis is a place where water can be found in an otherwise dry desert. It happens when the water table (the area below which the ground is saturated) comes to the surface, providing a welcome drink. The water may come to the surface in the form of a spring, and artificial oases have been made in some deserts by forcing groundwater up through wells. An oasis can be the size of a pond (typically surrounded by palm trees) or as large as the desert cities which have been built around these more fertile areas.

What have camels got in their humps

Not water! A camel's hump is made of fat. They are able to go for many days without eating or drinking, living off the fat stored in these humps. That is why they make such ideal animals for desert transport, earning them their famous nickname 'ships of the desert'.

What is the largest desert

The Sahara in North Africa is the world's biggest desert. It takes up 8 per cent of the world's land area and, contrary to popular belief, it is only covered in 30 per cent sand – the rest is gravel and other soils. Also impressive is the Arabian Desert, with 25 per cent of its area being unbroken sand.

Animals take advantage of an oasis in the desert.

FACT BYTES

Light rays travelling through the air in a desert pass from cooler, heavier air on the ground to lighter air further up. This causes the light to bend, and causes a 'shimmering' effect that looks like water. This is the 'mirage' that desert travellers may commonly experience when the air is warm enough.

EXTREME HEAT

AFRICA

The world's second largest continent is home to jungles and deserts, and some of the world's most amazing animals. The people live in large cities as well as in tribes that live by ancient traditions.

FACT FILE

AFRICA – Essential Fact File

- Area: 30,221,532 square kilometres (11,668,599 square miles)
- Number of countries: 57
- Largest country: Algeria (area – 2,381,741 square kilometres/ 919,595 square miles)
- Smallest country: Seychelles (area – 451 square kilometres/ 174 square miles)
- Longest river: The Nile – 6,650 kilometres (4,150 miles)
- Highest mountain: Mount Kilimanjaro in Tanzania, 5,895 metres (19,340 feet) above sea level

Sailing boats on the River Nile.

South Africa is fertile.

Crossing the Sahara.

What would you see travelling north to south ❓

Going from north to south, you would start at the beautiful blue Mediterranean Sea. That would give way to the burning sands of the Sahara Desert which go on for hundreds of miles. Around the middle of Africa, the scenery would change to thick rainforest with tall trees and lush vegetation. After that, you would be out on the savannah, the huge open plains where all the famous wild animals live. Finally, you would end up in South Africa, a rich and fertile country with huge farms that grow apples, oranges and grapes for making wine.

Africa is the world's second largest continent and is divided into 57 different countries, including archipelagoes, recognised states and territories.

Which animals live in Africa

On the savannah, you would see the following (amongst others) –

- Zebras
- Giraffes
- Elephants
- Lions
- Cheetahs
- Hyenas
- Hippopotamuses
- Rhinoceroses

Lion.

Zebra.

Rhino.

Sadly, many of the wonderful creatures have been hunted to the point that they now face extinction.

Which crops grow in Africa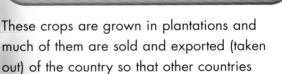

These crops are grown in plantations and much of them are sold and exported (taken out) of the country so that other countries can buy them.

- Cocoa • Tea
- Coffee • Fruit
- Cotton

Africa also exports massive quantities of palm oil which is used to make soap and margarine.

ASIA

Asia makes up nearly one-third of the world's total land mass. Both the world's highest and lowest points can be found here. Touched by four oceans and covering a huge area, the population is as diverse as the landscape.

FACT FILE

ASIA – Essential Fact File

- Area: 44,418,500 square kilometres (16,9885 square miles)

- Number of countries: 48

- Largest country: China

- Country with the largest number of people: China (followed by India)

- Important rivers: The Tigris, Euphrates, Indus, Ganges and Yangtze

- Highest mountain: Everest

- Fascinating feature: Lake Baikal in Russia. It is the deepest lake in the world and contains a fifth of all the fresh water on the planet!

What food is grown in Asia ❓

Rice is the staple diet of the people of Asia. It grows in layered, water-filled terraces called paddy fields. Wheat for making bread is also important.

The following crops are grown, then sold abroad – tea, cotton, rubber, jute, fruit and tobacco.

Which animals live in Asia ?

There are a large number of different animals living in Asia. The Asiatic (also called Indian) lion roams India, feeding on animals such as wild pig and sambar (an Asian deer). India is also home to 60 per cent of the world's tigers. The Asian elephant can be found across India and Sri Lanka and as far southeast as Sumatra. Moose roam the Arctic coast, and the famous giant panda lives in the mountains of central China.

A giant panda.

A tiger.

Why is the Dead Sea so called ?

Because nothing can live in it! This huge lake contains seven times as much salt as normal water. The salt in the Dead Sea makes it much denser than freshwater or normal salt water, so it can support your body and make you float! The Dead Sea is the lowest area on Earth's surface, at nearly 400 metres (1,312 feet) below sea level.

ASIA

Where did man evolve ?

Modern man (proper name Homo sapiens) evolved in Africa, but the first organised towns, cities and empires (called civilisations) developed in Asia. Amongst the earliest civilisations were those around the Tigris and Euphrates rivers in what is now Iraq, in ancient China and along the Indus Valley of modern Pakistan.

Floating away ...

ANTARCTICA

The fifth largest continent, Antarctica, has no countries or inhabitants. Scientists stay temporarily to discover more about this land of snow and ice. The South Pole is colder than the North Pole (in the Arctic) because it is surrounded by ice, whereas the North is enclosed by water which has an insulating effect. The warmest it ever gets is 0°C (32°F)!

FACT FILE

Antarctica – Essential Fact File

- Area: 13,824,000 square kilometres (5,400,000 square miles)

- Number of countries: None!

- Thickness of the ice: 2,500–4,800 metres (8,202–15,748 feet)

- Abundance of ice: Ninety per cent of the world's ice is found in the Antarctic

- Coldest temperature: –89.2°C (–128.6°F) recorded in 1983

- Animal life: Penguins, seals and whales

- Continent is made from two massive ice plates, the east and west Antarctic Ice Sheets.

- The 'poles' are simply names for the top and bottom of our planet

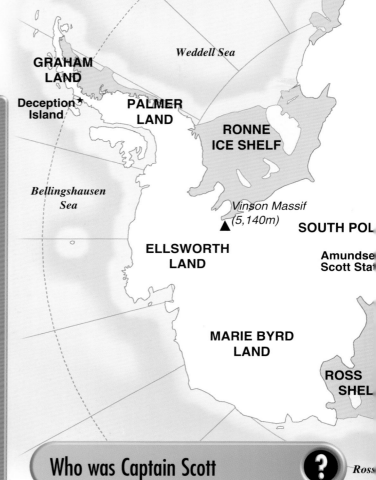

GRAHAM LAND

Weddell Sea

Deception Island

PALMER LAND

RONNE ICE SHELF

Bellingshausen Sea

Vinson Massif ▲ (5,140m)

SOUTH POL

ELLSWORTH LAND

Amundse Scott Stat

MARIE BYRD LAND

ROSS SHEL

Who was Captain Scott ❓

Ross

In 1912, two teams of explorers, one from Norway and one from Britain, raced each other to the South Pole. The Norwegian team, led by Roald Amundsen, got there first. The British team, led by Robert Falcon Scott, arrived at the Pole only to find the Norwegian flag already flying there. Overcome by exhaustion and hunger, Scott's team didn't survive the journey back – they all died in the frozen wilderness.

Captain Scott.

A huge hole appears above Antarctica each summer.

EEN MAUD LAND

ENDERBY LAND

Davis Sea

Antarctica

PRINCESS ELIZABETH LAND

★ **Vostok**

*ount Kirkpatrick
,528m)*

WILKES LAND

★ **McMurdo Station**

THE DRY VALLEYS

SOUTH MAGNETIC POLE

Blue whales breathe through blowholes, which can be heard for miles around the Antarctic.

What kind of animals live in the Antarctic ?

All the big ones! The elephant seal, which is over 6 metres (20 feet) long, lives here, along with the grey seal and the leopard seal. The emperor penguin (1.1 metres/3.8 feet tall) is the largest of the penguin species found in the Antarctic. Amongst the various whales in the sea is the gigantic blue whale, the largest living mammal on Earth.

The leopard seal is so called because of its distinctive markings. Its only natural predator is the killer whale.

Emperor penguins are social birds who huddle, taking turns to move to the centre for warmth.

Is there a hole above Antarctica ?

Man's excessive use of gases and chemicals is thought to have weakened the ozone layer (which protects us from the Sun's heat). Scientists have observed a large 'hole' in the atmosphere above Antarctica, in the months of September and October. However, it is simply the very low temperatures in the atmosphere over the area that cause this. When summer arrives (December to January) the air above Antarctica is mixed with the world's atmosphere and the hole 'repairs' itself. Worryingly though, the 'hole', first observed in the 1970s, has become bigger each year.

AUSTRALASIA

Every part of Australasia, the smallest continent, is surrounded by ocean. This affects the climate here. Australia is generally mild all year round, whereas Papua New Guinea is hot and tropical. New Zealand's warm and wet climate makes it very fertile (although parts of the South Island can experience snow all year round!).

FACT FILE

AUSTRALASIA – Essential Fact File

- Area (Australia only): 7,687,000 square kilometres (2,70272 square miles)

- States (Australia only): New South Wales, Victoria, Queensland, South Australia, Tasmania, Northern Territory and Western Australia

- Highest mountain: Puncak Jaya, New Guinea – 5,030 metres (16,503 feet)

- Animal life: Kangaroos, wombats, koalas

- Exports: Coal, gold, meat, wool

- Features: Uluru (also known as Ayers Rock), Great Barrier Reef

Uluru.

PAPUA NEW GUINEA

Darwin ★

WESTERN AUSTRALIA

Macdonnell Ra

Great Sandy Desert

Uluru

Gibson Desert

Great Victoria Desert

Nullarbor Plain

Perth ★

What does Australia produce

Much of Australia contains vast swathes of barren desert. The population tends to live in cities around the coast. The rest of the country consists of grassy plains and highlands which are ideal for keeping cattle and sheep. Australia has millions of sheep – the country produces one third of all the wool used in the whole world. New Zealand is also a great sheep-rearing country, but their better-quality grazing land means that the animals are raised for meat which is frozen and sold abroad.

Who are the Aborigines and the Maoris

Aborigines are the native people of Australia. Maoris are the native people of New Zealand. Both lived in their respective countries for thousands of years before the arrival of white European settlers. It is believed that Aborigines made their way from Asia at least 30,000 years ago. Today, they make up approximately 1.5 per cent of the Australian population.

Cairns ★

Great Barrier Reef

THERN TERRITORY

STRALIA

QUEENSLAND

Great Dividing Range

Simpson Desert

TH AUSTRALIA

Brisbane ★

NEW SOUTH WALES

Sydney ★

★ Adelaide

Canberra ★

VICTORIA

Melbourne ★

Australian capital territory

TASMANIA
Hobart ★

North Cape

Auckland .

NEW ZEALAND

★ **Wellington**

. Dunedin

What are the famous sights

The Great Barrier Reef is the largest coral reef in the world, extending over 2,000 kilometres (1,243 miles) off the northern shore of Queensland, Australia. Coral is a living stone made up of billions of tiny animals called coral polyps. This beautiful underwater landscape is in danger of dying off due to pollution in the water.

Uluru (also known as Ayers Rock) is the biggest monolith (single block of stone) in the world. Found in the desert in the centre of Australia it rises 348 metres (1,142 feet) above the ground.

When did European settlers reach Australasia

Australia and New Zealand were both discovered by a Royal Navy explorer from Yorkshire, England, called Captain James Cook. He landed in New Zealand in 1768 and in Australia in 1770, claiming both for Britain. Afterwards, the British government used Australia as a place to send convicted criminals, a policy known as transportation.

AUSTRALASIA

EUROPE

The sixth largest continent, Europe, is formed from many countries, each with its own culture. This makes it a diverse place to visit.

FACT FILE

EUROPE – Essential Fact File

- Area: 10,532,000 square kilometres (3,86102 square miles)

- Number of countries: 50

- Longest river: the Volga in Russia, 3,692 kilometres (2,294 miles) long

- Highest mountain: Mount Elbrus, also in Russia, 5,642 metres (18,510 feet) high

- Largest city by area: Paris

What is the climate like in Europe ?

In the north, countries like Norway and Finland receive a lot of snow and have frozen territory inside the Arctic Circle. To the south, countries like Spain, Italy and Greece bask in hot sunshine for many months, and are holiday destination favourites. Eastern countries such as Hungary have warm summers but much colder winters.

Mediterranean heat.

Frozen territory!

Which is the biggest country ?

Russia is the biggest country in Europe. The smallest is The Vatican, the Pope's palace in Rome. Even though it is only 0.44 square kilometres (0.17 square miles), it is classified as a separate country!

Which city has the most people ?

The most highly populated cities in Europe include Moscow in Russia, Istanbul in Turkey and London in the UK.

FINLAND

Helsinki ★

Stockholm ★ *Baltic Sea*

★Tallinn
ESTONIA

SWEDEN

Riga ★ LATVIA

★Copenhagen

Volga

LITHUANIA

RUSS. FED.

★Kaunas

Minsk ★

BELARUS

POLAND

erlin ★

Warsaw ★

Kiev ★

UKRAINE

★Prague

ZECH REPUBLIC

Dnieper

SLOVAKIA

★Bratislava

MOLDOVA

Vienna ★

AUSTRIA

★Budapest

HUNGARY

★Chisinau

Ljubljana ★

★Zagreb

ROMANIA

LOVENIA

CROATIA

★Belgrade

BOSNIA &

HERZEGOVINA SERBIA

★Bucharest

Danube ★Sarajevo

driatic Sea

ALY

MONTENEGRO

BULGARIA

★KOSOVO ★Sofia

Podgorica ★

★Pristina

Tirane ★

★Skopje

MACEDONIA

Rome ★

ALBANIA

GREECE

★Athens

Sicily

CYPRUS

editerranean Sea

Crete

How has Europe changed

Europe is a peninsula (a piece of land that sticks out, joined at one end to another piece of land). Its physical shape has remained the same over the centuries, but the borders of the countries change all the time. Since ancient times, Europe has been the continent of empires. The Greeks, the Romans, the French, the Germans, the Spanish and the British (to name but a few) have marched their armies into other countries to take them over and impose their way of life. Europe has a history of warfare.

A Roman warrior – the Roman Empire began in Italy and spread into many other countries.

What does Mediterranean mean

The name Mediterranean means 'in the middle of the land'. In ancient times, it was literally the centre of the known world. Western culture began here with the Greeks and Romans and we still follow many of the laws and customs that they laid down. In particular, we use their form of government in which people choose their leaders by voting. This is known as democracy.

EUROPE

NORTH AMERICA

The third largest continent is formed from the larger countries of Canada, Mexico and the United States, the countries of Central America and the Caribbean islands. The land is diverse, from the harsh conditions of the Arctic Circle to the tropical beaches of Florida. There's even some desert!

FACT FILE

NORTH AMERICA – Essential Fact File

- Area: 24,709,000 square kilometres (9,540,000 square miles)

- Number of countries: 23

- Main mountains: The Rockies

- Main rivers: Mississippi–Missouri, St Lawrence, Rio Grande and Colorado

- Main lakes: Superior, Michigan, Huron, Erie and Ontario (The Great Lakes)

- Most famous feature: Niagara Falls

North America covers 24,709,000 square kilometres (9,540,000 square miles) – slightly larger than Brazil and about half the size of Russia.

Christopher Columbus.

Who was Christopher Columbus

This Italian explorer was credited with discovering the Americas. He made four voyages, landing on the American mainland in 1498. He thought he had reached India. That is why the big islands south of Florida are called the West Indies and Native Americans have, until recently, been known as Indians. However, it is now known that the Vikings were the first Europeans to reach America, having sailed there several centuries earlier.

What is there to see in North America

Everything is said to be big in America and it certainly has its own share of 'biggest and best' –

• Lake Superior is the world's largest freshwater lake

• Greenland is the world's largest island

• The world's tallest trees are found in California

• The Rocky Mountains are the world's second longest mountain range

• The Mississippi–Missouri River is the fourth longest river in the world

The Rockies.

The Mississippi river.

What are the Great Lakes

The five lakes near the border of Canada and the United States are really vast inland seas which cover an area of 1,200 kilometres (750 miles). In terms of volume, the largest is Lake Superior, followed by Michigan, Huron, Ontario and Erie.

What are the famous sites

Niagara Falls is a spectacular waterfall that sees almost half a million tonnes of water plunge over a 50 metre (164 feet) drop every minute! This massive amount of water comes from the Great Lakes just to the north.

The Grand Canyon is the deepest gorge in the world. (A gorge is a deep valley cut by a river.) Created by the Colorado river in Arizona, the Canyon has some breathtaking scenery and, like Niagara Falls, is a famous tourist attraction.

The Grand Canyon.

NORTH AMERICA

39

SOUTH AMERICA

South America is the fourth largest continent, and its countries display a great variety of climates. There's the wet, tropical Amazon rainforest in Brazil, the humid subtropical temperatures of Argentina and the dry mountain air of Peru.

FACT FILE

SOUTH AMERICA – Essential Fact File

- Area: 17,840,000 square kilometres (6,890,000 square miles)

- Number of countries: 12

- Biggest country: Brazil (covers half of the whole continent)

- Main mountains: the Andes

- Main rivers: the Amazon, Orinoco and the joint River Plate–Paraguay–Parana

- Famous feature: the Amazon rainforest, the Amazon River and the Angel Falls waterfall

The Angel Falls, in Venezuela, the world's highest uninterrupted waterfall.

The rainforests of South America are home to many species of wildlife, including the parrot, sloth and tarantula.

Barranquilla

Medellin

Bogota

COLOMBIA

Quito

ECUADOR

PERU

Pacific Ocean

Lima

Andes Mountains

What exactly is a rainforest ?

In rainforests, lots of trees grow close together, the tops of which are called crowns. Some trees grow to 61 metres (200 feet) and form the upper canopy, which is home to many types of wildlife, including the sloth (above). Shorter trees, which form the other layers of the canopy, help to block out the light, so that relatively little grows on the rainforest floor. Rainforests are different to jungles, which receive a lot of sunlight, and have areas of dense growth on the ground (often found near swamps).

San

What is special about the Andes ?

It is the longest mountain range in the world. The mountains start up in the north in Colombia and run right down the Pacific coast to Patagonia, a distance of about 8,000 kilometres (4,970 miles). Their highest point is Mount Aconcagua in Argentina which is 6,960 metres (22,837 feet) above sea level.

What is the Amazon basin

The Amazon River starts in the Andes mountains and flows right through South America for a distance of 6,450 kilometres (4,007 miles). Over the centuries, this mighty river has carved out a wide, flat area either side which is known as its basin. Much of the Amazon basin is covered by tropical rainforest.

The Amazon starts in the Andes.

What does Brazil produce

The flat-to-rolling land and mainly tropical climate leads to the successful growth of coffee, cocoa, sugar and soya beans, and Brazil exports a lot of these products. The majority of coffee beans produced for export come from the arabica bush, which bears fruit containing two seeds.

Why are rare animals in danger

In many parts of South America, the cutting and burning of trees takes place in order to clear land for livestock to graze and crops to be planted. This process is known as deforestation. Once these areas of the rainforest have been cleared, the animals and plants lose their habitat and may become extinct. There is pressure on these countries to gain income through other methods, and to leave the natural world intact.

Deforestation.

SOUTH AMERICA

Caracas
Valencia
Orinoco
VENEZUELA
Georgetown
Paramaribo
SURINAME
Cayenne
GUYANA
FRENCH GUIANA
Negro
Belem
Manaus
Amazon
Fortaleza
Madeira
Recife
Tocantins
Rio São Francisco
BRAZIL
BOLIVIA
Salvador
La Paz
Goiania
Brasilia
Sucre
Mato Grosso
Plateau
Belo Horizonte
PARAGUAY
Rio de Janeiro
Sao Paulo
Asuncion
Curitiba
Parana
Paraguay
ARGENTINA
Porto Alegre
Rosario
URUGUAY
Buenos Aires
Montevideo
Atlantic Ocean
FALKLAND ISLANDS
Stanley
Tierra Del Fuego

SUN AND MOON

The Moon orbits Earth, and Earth orbits the Sun. When these paths cross, we can witness wonderful sights. Even our little Moon has some control over us ...

How does the Moon cause tides

As the Moon orbits Earth, its gravitational field pulls Earth's water towards it. Earth is turning at the same time, interrupting the pull. This causes two high and two low tides every day. High tide is when the ocean flows as far inland as possible, low tide is when it flows as far as it can from land.

Why does the Moon appear to be the same size as the Sun

The Moon is 382,000 kilometres (237,364 miles) from Earth, and can be reached by space rockets. The Sun, however, is 149,598,020 kilometres (92,584,300 miles) away. So, although the Moon is 400 times smaller than the Sun, they seem the same size in the sky.

The Moon is much closer to Earth than the Sun.

What are solar and lunar eclipses

A solar eclipse occurs when the Moon passes in front of the Sun, casting its shadow on part of Earth. A lunar eclipse is the opposite – Earth passes in front of the Sun and casts its shadow on part of the Moon. A rare total eclipse happens when Earth and the Moon line up, blocking the Sun temporarily.

What is the Sun's corona

During a total solar eclipse, the Moon passes exactly in front of the Sun and, for a few minutes, you can see only the Sun's halo of glowing gases, called the corona (meaning 'crown'). Scientists are unsure why these rays at the edge of the Sun, shooting off into the atmosphere, are actually hotter than the Sun's surface (the photosphere).

How big is the Moon's shadow

During a solar eclipse, the dark shadow that the Moon casts on Earth's surface is a circle about 270 kilometres (168 miles) across. It is called the umbra. A much lighter shadow (about 3,000 kilometres/1,864 miles across) surrounds the umbra.

The Moon casts a shadow called the umbra.

WARNING

You should not look at an eclipse with a telescope, the naked eye, or even through sunglasses as the Sun's light could cause damage to your eyes. However, it is possible to view an eclipse safely through a pin-hole camera.

FACT BYTES

An eclipse viewed from Earth lasts for only a few minutes. From the air, however, its time can be greatly extended by following the eclipse round the world in a fast-moving aircraft.

SUN AND MOON

NATURAL WONDERS

Our planet has many beautiful places which have breathtaking natural features and awe-inspiring scenery. Here's a look at the top six which maybe you'll be lucky enough to visit one day ...

The Victoria Falls

On the border of Zimbabwe and Zambia, the falls are known locally as the 'Mosi-oa-Tunya' ('smoke that thunders'). The seven waterfalls occur when the Zambezi river plunges 108 metres (354 feet) down several series of basalt gorges.

Mauna Loa

This is the world's largest active volcano. It is so large that it takes up half the area of Hawaii. The top point is a massive 4,169 metres (13,679 feet) high. The large crater at the top, named Mokuaweoweo Caldera, can be clearly seen from space! Scientists believe it started to form nearly one million years ago.

Great Barrier Reef

The world's largest coral reef, is an underwater world of astonishing colour and beauty. It is located off the coast of northeast Australia and is built by billions of tiny organisms, as well as being home to a wide diversity of life – from fish to turtles.

Mount Everest **4**

Arguably the world's greatest natural wonder, it is the tallest of the many snow-capped Himalayan peaks that seem to reach up and touch the sky.

Yellowstone National Park **5**

This huge protected area in America mainly consists of lakes, mountain ranges, rivers and canyons. It is also home to the biggest natural geysers in the world which shoot scalding hot water into the sky at regular intervals.

The Grand Canyon **6**

Also in America, the scenery here is so awesome that you feel small just looking at it! The gorge was carved out by the Colorado river, in Arizona, around 17 million years ago.

GLOSSARY

Aborigine
A native of Australia who was living there when European settlers arrived.

Aftershocks
Tremors following an earthquake.

Arid
Description of a place that has little or no rain.

Atmosphere
The gassy area surrounding Earth, split into five layers.

Aurora borealis
The 'northern lights' – spectacular light displays mainly seen in the night skies of the most northern hemisphere.

Avalanche
A large fall of snow and ice down a mountain.

Basin
Where a river and its tributaries join together and are 'captured'.

Beaufort Scale
An international scale used to measure wind speeds.

Billion
A billion is a thousand million. Written as a number it is 1,000,000,000.

Brackish
Slightly salty water – usually found where a river meets the sea.

Climate
The type of weather that is typical (long term) of an area.

Condensation
The process in which gas becomes compressed into either a liquid or solid state.

Crater
The cone-shaped mountain built up by a volcano, often with an open top. If the volcano is still active, lava will bubble in the crater.

Dead Sea
The lowest area of water on Earth's surface, so full of salt that it cannot support life.

Delta
The flat area at the end of a river, which has divided into a number of smaller distributaries.

Drought
A long period of low rainfall.

Eclipse
The total or partial obscuring of one celestial body by another.

Electromagnetic waves
The energy which is produced by an electromagnetic field.

Empire
A group of people and land under the rule of a single person or state.

Epicentre
The point immediately above the origin of an earthquake.

Estuary
Where a river reaches the end of its journey – flowing into a river or lake at a slow speed.

Evaporation
The process by which something more dense changes into something less dense (like a liquid to a gas).

Export
Food, raw materials and manufactured goods that are sold to other countries to make money.

Extinct and Extinction
When a species of animal is about to die out and disappear for ever, it is said to be facing extinction. When this terrible event finally happens, the animal has become extinct.

Faculae
Bright clouds of helium above areas where sunspots form.

Galaxy
A group of stars and planets forming a part of the universe.

Geyser
A spring that discharges steam and hot water.

Global warming
Because of pollution, Earth's atmosphere is getting warmer. This may have serious consequences in the very near future.

Gorge
A deep valley formed by a river.

Gravity
This is the natural force that presses down on the surface of Earth, keeping everything in place.

Ice shelf

Found at the Poles, a thick block of ice attached to the land which sticks out and floats into the sea.

Inuit

A native of the Arctic.

Irrigation

The use of water from rivers and lakes to make crops grow.

Jute

Yellow-flowered plants, grown for their strong fibres which can be made into rope and other such products.

Lava

The hot liquid magma spewing from the top or sides of a volcano.

Magma

Hot molten rock within Earth's crust which becomes solid rock if it reaches Earth's surface.

Magnetic field

A field of force surrounding a permanent magnet.

Maori

A Polynesian native living in New Zealand and the Cook Islands.

Molecules

Everything in the world is made of atoms. When these atoms bond together in different ways, the resulting compounds are called molecules.

Monolith

A large block of stone.

Ozone layer

A layer of molecules that forms in the stratosphere. Good at absorbing ultraviolet radiation, it protects life on Earth.

Paddyfields

Layered, water-filled terraces, used for growing rice.

Peninsula

A piece of land that sticks out, joined at one end to another area of land.

Population

The number of inhabitants (usually people) living in a particular place.

Precipitation

Any weather such as rain, snow, sleet or dew, caused by the condensation of water in the atmosphere.

Rainforest

A thick forest found in areas that have heavy rainfall.

Reef

A ridge of rock, sand, coral etc, the top of which lies just under the sea's surface.

Reservoir

A lake which collects and stores water for people to use.

Richter Scale

An international scale used to measure the strength of earthquakes.

Sandstorm

A swirling mass of sand, whipped up by the wind.

Seismic

Relating to, or caused by, earthquakes or Earth tremors.

Solar flares

Bright loops of hot gas emerging from areas of the Sun where sunspots are present.

Solar system

This is the name of the group of eight planets, including Earth, that go round the Sun.

Staple diet

A food of prime importance, in terms of consumption and trade.

Static electricity

Electrical energy that builds up in a certain place rather than being 'on the move' like other electricity.

Summit

The highest point of a mountain.

Sunspot

A dark area on the Sun's surface.

Supercontinent

A huge piece of land thought to have split into smaller pieces which now form the seven continents.

Tributary

A stream, river or glacier that feeds on another of these.

Umbra

A shadow cast by the Moon on the surface of Earth.

Water cycle

Water circulation, via evaporation, precipitation and condensation.

GLOSSARY

INDEX

Acknowledgements

Main illustrations by Mike Atkinson.

Key:Top – t; middle – m; bottom – b; left – l; right – r;

1: Stephen Sweet, SGA. **2:** (t) Stephen Sweet/SGA; (m) Corel. **3:** NASA. **5:** Image 100. **6:** TTAT. **8–9:** Sean Milne. **10:** Digital Stock. **11:** Topham Picture Point. **12:** (m) Image Stock; (b) Corel; Sean Milne. **13:** Muti Maps. **14:** Sean Milne. **15:** (t) TTAT; (b) Rex Features. **16:** James King-Holmes/Science Photo Library. **18:** TopThat! **19:** Topham picture Point. **20:** (m) TTAT; (b) Corbis Images. **21:** (t) NASA; (b) Corbis Images. **22:** TTAT. **23:** Corbis Images. **25:** (l) Multi Maps; (r) Corbis Images. **26:** Multi Maps. **27:** Corel. **28:** (m) Corel; (bl) Flat Earth; (br) Topham Picture Point. **29:** Multi Maps. **30:** Digital Stock. **31:** Multi Maps; (b) Topham Picture Point. **32:** (m) Photo Alto; (b) Topham Picture Point. **33:** Multi Maps. **34:** (m) Multi Maps; (b) Digital Stock. **35:** Corel. **36:** Photo Alto. **37:** Multi Maps.**38:** Multi Maps. **39:** (tl) Digital Stock; (tr) Photo Disc; (b) Photo Disc. **40:** (m) Mutli Maps; (b) Topham Picture Point. **41:** Topham Picture Point. **43:** Photo Disc.